We know from Luke 2:8–20 that t
the shepherds the good n

Trace the letters A and a.

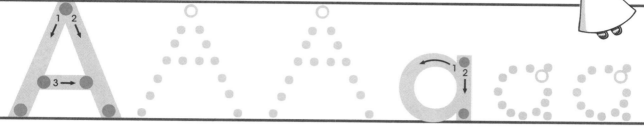

Circle the letters A and a.

A d a A D e F

B a A e a D A

Color the pictures that begin with the "a" sound.

"A" is for Angel from whom the shepherds first heard the news.

1

We know from Psalm 29:11 that we receive
the blessing of peace from God.

Trace the letters B and b.

B B B b b b

Circle the letters B and b.

B e b K n b B

S b B a b M g

Color the pictures that begin with the "b" sound.

"B" is for Blessings which we receive from God.

We know from Romans 5:8
that Christ died for us.

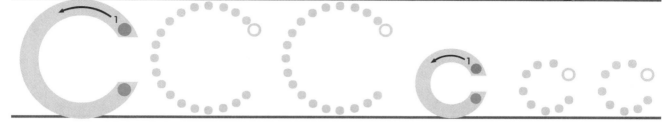

Trace the letters C and c.

C c c c c c

Circle the letters C and c.

K C m c S c L

C Z c N C h c

Color the pictures that begin with the "c" sound.

"C" is for Christ who died on the cross for you.

We know from Proverbs 3:5-6 to trust
the Lord with our whole heart.

Trace the letters D and d.

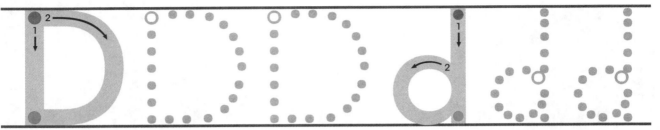

Circle the letters D and d.

D y d m Q D d

H d w D d e S

Color the pictures that begin with the "d" sound.

"D" is for Devotion which we have for God.

We know from Psalm 103:17 that God's
love for us is everlasting.

Trace the letters E and e.

E E E e e e

Circle the letters E and e.

R e z H E k e

E t E e Q e C

Color the pictures that begin with the "e" sound.

"E" is for Everlasting which is the wonderful love of God.

5

We know from John 14:23 that if we love Jesus he will
come and make his home with us.

Trace the letters F and f.

Circle the letters F and f.

F j f u F f K

R e F B f F A

Color the pictures that begin with the "f" sound.

"F" is for Friend which Jesus wants to be.

We know from Colossians 3:12–15 that we are God's chosen people, dearly loved.

Review the letters A, B, C, D, E, and F.

Aa Bb Cc Dd Ee Ff

Draw a line connecting the picture to its beginning letter sound.

A

C

F

B

E

D

Bible Alphabet Fun

We know from John 3:16 that God loved us so much that he gave his one and only son to die for our sins.

Trace the letters G and g.

G G G g g g

Circle the letters G and g.

G h V g G W g

d F G l j g G

Color the pictures that begin with the "g" sound.

"G" is for God who gave his one and only son.

We know from John 14:1-4 that Jesus is preparing a place for us in heaven where we will be with God forever.

Trace the letters H and h.

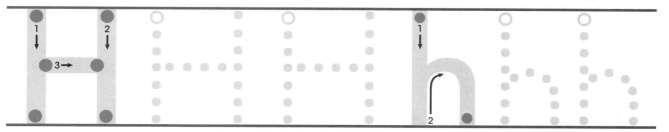

Circle the letters H and h.

T H j O h H e

H f X h H r h

Color the pictures that begin with the "h" sound.

"H" is for Heaven where Jesus is preparing a place for you.

© School Zone Publishing Company 02124

We know from Psalm 136 that God's
love will last forever.

Trace the letters I and i.

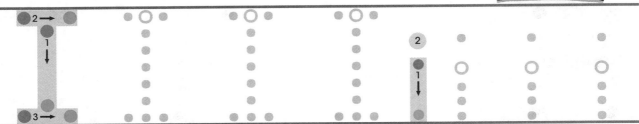

Circle the letters I and i.

I   o   R   i   I   S   c

M   i   I   H   k   I   i

Color the pictures that begin with the "i" sound.

"I" is for Incredible which describes God's love for you.

We know from 1 Thessalonians 4:13–18 that Jesus
will come again to take us to heaven.

Trace the letters J and j.

J J J j j j

Circle the letters J and j.

J Y r j E J g

j d J w j Z J

Color the pictures that begin with the "j" sound.

"J" is for Jesus who died and rose again.

Bible Alphabet Fun

We know from Galatians 4:7 that we are God's
children and heirs to his kingdom.

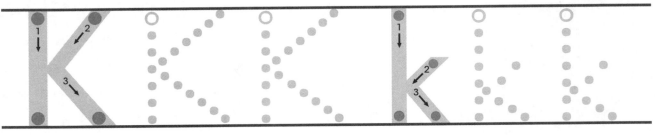

Trace the letters K and k.

○ Circle the letters K and k.

m k h K k l W

K G k Q e k K

Color the pictures that begin with the "k" sound.

"K" is for Kingdom where God has made you his heir.

Bible Alphabet Fun

We know from 2 Corinthians 4:16 that we are
renewed in God's love every single day.

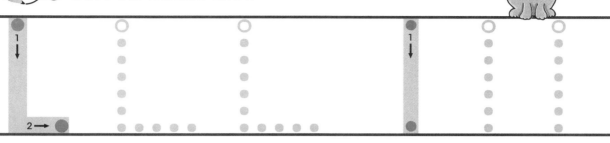

Trace the letters L and l.

Circle the letters L and l.

L N k l L r l
w L Y E t l L

Color the pictures that begin with the "l" sound.

"L" is for Love which God gives every day.

Bible Alphabet Fun

We know from Luke 2:4-7 that Jesus was born
in a stable and laid in a manger.

Trace the letters M and m.

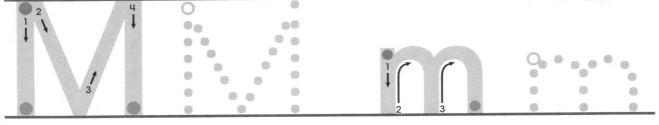

Circle the letters M and m.

n M L o m Z M

M w m c M m T

Color the pictures that begin with the "m" sound.

"M" is for Manger where Jesus was placed.

We know from Colossians 3:17 to give thanks to God
through Jesus for all he has done for us.

Review the letters G, H, I, J, K, L, and M.

Gg Hh Ii Jj Kk Ll Mm

Draw a line connecting the picture to its beginning letter sound.

G

J

L

H

M

I

K

We know from Luke 10:27 that Jesus wants us to
love our neighbor as we love ourselves.

Trace the letters N and n.

Circle the letters N and n.

D n N u R N w
N m O n N n T

Color the pictures that begin with the "n" sound.

"N" is for Neighbor whom Jesus tells us to love.

Bible Alphabet Fun

We know from Romans 12:1-2 that we are to trust God to guide our lives so that all we do is an offering.

Trace the letters O and o.

O O O O o oo

Circle the letters O and o.

O P N o O z o

B o O r V O L

Color the pictures that begin with the "o" sound.

Bible Alphabet Fun

We know from Psalm 34:1 to always have
praises to God on our lips.

Trace the letters P and p.

P P P P p p p

Circle the letters P and p.

L H p P o w P

p b P Q p u

Color the pictures that begin with the "p" sound.

"P" is for Praise to worship God.

We know from Psalm 46:10 that God tells us
to be still and know he is our God.

Trace the letters Q and q.

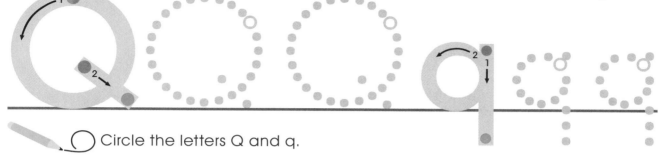

Circle the letters Q and q.

Q R t q Q u G

q b Q E h q Q

Color the pictures that begin with the "q" sound.

"Q" is for Quiet to hear God's voice.

Bible Alphabet Fun

We know from Philippians 4:4 to rejoice in the Lord always.

Trace the letters R and r.

R R R R R R   r r r r

Circle the letters R and r.

m R r b r e R

s t A r R r P

Color the pictures that begin with the "r" sound.

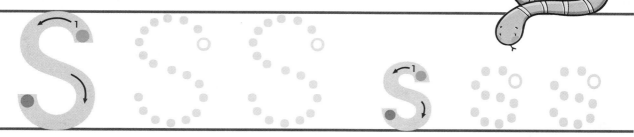

Trace the letters S and s.

S   S   S   s   s   s

Circle the letters S and s.

S   s   u   X   s   h   S

A   S   z   s   e   S   M

Color the pictures that begin with the "s" sound.

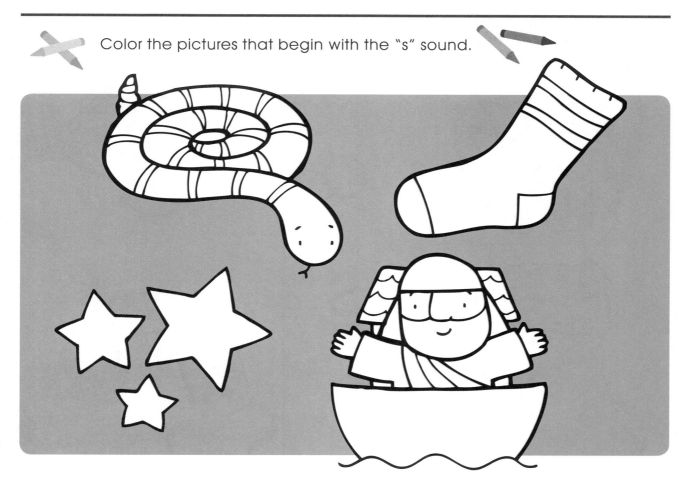

"S" is for Savior the Lord of all.

Bible Alphabet Fun

We know from John 1:14–17 that we receive one blessing after another by the richness of grace we have through Jesus.

Review the letters N, O, P, Q, R, and S.

N n O o P p Q q R r S s

Draw a line connecting the picture to its beginning letter sound.

N

R

P

Q

S

O

Bible Alphabet Fun   © School Zone Publishing Company 02124

We know from Hebrews 12:28 that God's
kingdom cannot be shaken.

Trace the letters T and t.

Circle the letters T and t.

y T n t W T t

T g k R T t O

Color the pictures that begin with the "t" sound.

"T" is for Trusting God's love.

Bible Alphabet Fun

We know from Psalm 139 that God knows and
understands everything about us.

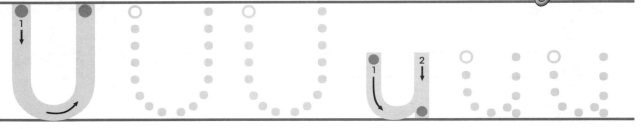

Trace the letters U and u.

Circle the letters U and u.

U b u z o U u

N u W U Y u L

Color the pictures that begin with the "u" sound.

"U" is for Understands which Jesus does every day.

Bible Alphabet Fun   © School Zone Publishing Company 02124

We know from 1 John 5:1–5 that Jesus is the one who has victory over the world.

 Trace the letters V and v.

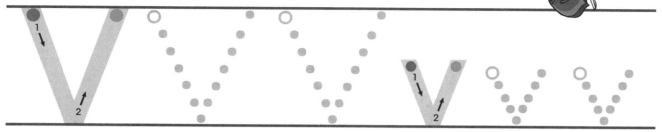

Circle the letters V and v.

R V h v V L e

v x V w o V v

Color the pictures that begin with the "v" sound.

"V" is for Victory which we have in Jesus.

Bible Alphabet Fun

We know from 1 John 1:5–7 that Jesus wants us
to walk with him in his light.

Trace the letters W and w.

Circle the letters W and w.

W w b S W i w

x r W h w W a

Color the pictures that begin with the "w" sound.

"W" is for Walk which is what we do with Jesus.

We know from 1 Corinthians 6:14 that the same God who raised Jesus from the grave will also raise us up.

Trace the letters X and x.

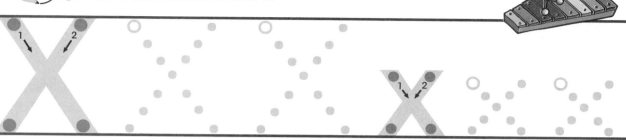

Circle the letters X and x.

Z   u   X   n   x   p   X

X   x   A   X   c   x   S

Color the pictures that begin with the "x" sound.

"X" is for eX-cited which is how we feel about our faith.

We know from John 10:1–18 that Jesus knows each
of us by name and that we belong to him.

Trace the letters Y and y.

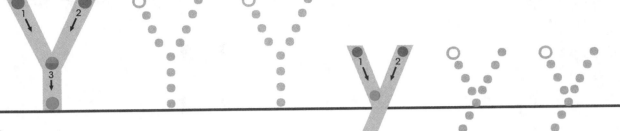

Circle the letters Y and y.

Y f y H Y y o

B Y s y m d Y

Color the pictures that begin with the "y" sound.

"y" is for You whom Jesus loves very much.

We know from Romans 12:11 that we are to never lose
our zeal, which means eagerness for our faith.

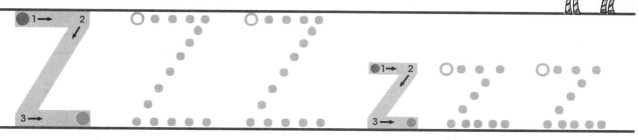

Trace the letters Z and z.

Circle the letters Z and z.

Z K z r s Z z

F b o z Z p Z

Color the pictures that begin with the "z" sound.

Bible Alphabet Fun

We know from John 15:1–11 that by staying connected
to Jesus our joy will be made complete.

Review the letters T, U, V, W, X, Y, and Z.

Tt Uu Vv Ww Xx Yy Zz

Draw a line connecting the picture to its beginning letter sound.

T

X

W

U

Z

Y

V

We know from Psalm 97:1-6 that the whole earth is glad
because God's love reigns.

Trace each letter of the alphabet. Then, draw
a line to connect the uppercase letter to its matching
lowercase letter.

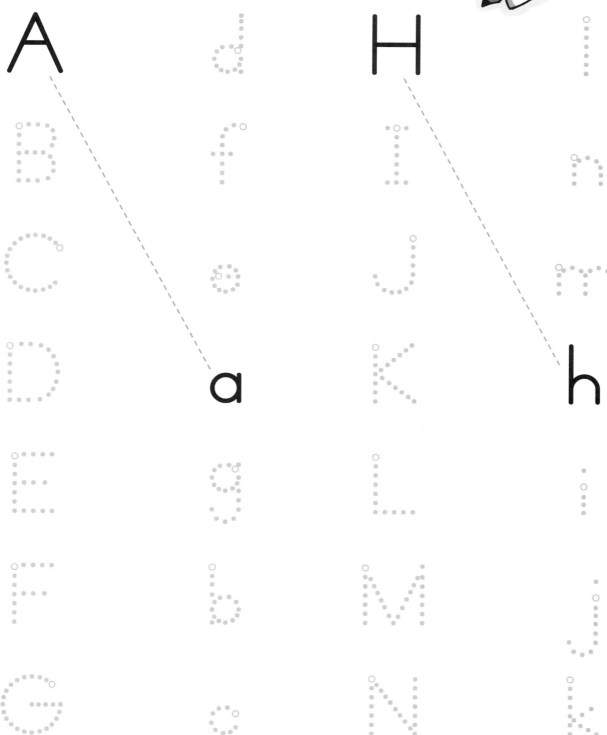

Bible Alphabet Fun

We know from Romans 11:33 that God's love is so big it would be impossible for us to trace around.

Trace each letter of the alphabet. Then, draw a line to connect the uppercase letter to its matching lowercase letter.

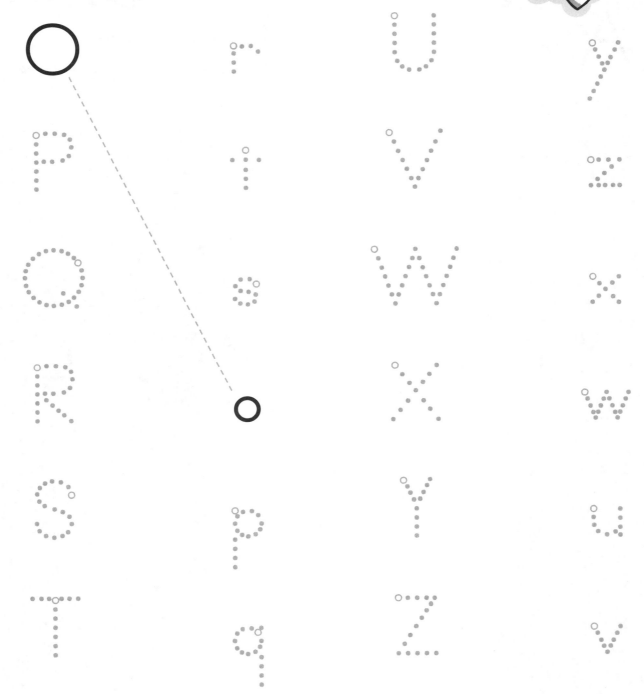

Bible Alphabet Fun 02124